100 PRAYERS FOR WRITERS

Creative Fuel for Inspired Work

Books by Bob Hostetler
(a partial list)

Nonfiction

*Don't Check Your Brains at the Door**
Holy Moses (And Other Adventures in Vertical Living)
*Right From Wrong**
American Idols
Quit Going to Church
How to Survive the End of the World
Life Stinks...And Then You Die
Falling in Love with God
The Red Letter Life
The Red Letter Prayer Life
The Bard and the Bible
The Shakespeare Devotional

Fiction

*The Love Killer**
They Call Me AWOL
*The Truth Slayers**
*The Deceivers**
*The Truth Twisters**
The Bone Box
Northkill†
The Return†

Children's Books

Don't Close Your Eyes
I Dream a Dream for You

Poetry

Jordan River Anthology

*coauthored with Josh McDowell
†coauthored with J. M. Hochstetler

100 PRAYERS FOR WRITERS

Creative Fuel for Inspired Work

BOB HOSTETLER

CHRISTIAN WRITERS INSTITUTE

100 Prayers for Writers: Creative Fuel for Inspired Work

Printed in the United States of America.

Published by The Christian Writers Institute, LLC, Phoenix, AZ USA.

Visit The Christian Writers Institute at *www.ChristianWritersInstitute.com*.

ISBN: 978-1-62184-250-7 (printed softcover)

ISBN: 978-1-62184-251-4 (ebook)

Cover design and interior layout by Collin Smith Creative (*collinsmithcreative.com*)

Table of Contents

A Short Introduction

Many years ago, when the world was young, after I'd written and published my first seventeen or eighteen books, I was totally spent as a writer. I'd been through a 3-year process of revision and revulsion on one book that had left me doubting my ability, and drained of all enthusiasm for writing.
So I prayed. I sometimes do that when I get desperate...and there's nothing good on television.

And God sent me manna from heaven in the form of an assignment to work on a project called The Prayer Bible. For the next couple months, I spent my workdays praying through the second half of the Old Testament, praying God's Word back to him, and writing those prayers, a process that not only revived me and stoked my prayer life...I believe it saved my writing ministry.

It changed the writing process for me. It made prayer an indispensable part of the writing process for me, so much so that I don't know how I ever wrote anything before I came to see the absolute connectedness that exists between prayer and writing.

It shouldn't be a surprise to any of us, of course...God was talking about writing as much as anything when he spoke to Zerubbabel through Zechariah:

"Not by might nor by power, but by my Spirit," says the Lord Almighty (Zechariah 4:6).

If I truly believed that, why would I try to write anything in my own strength, apart from prayerful dependence on God? Why would you?

I realize, of course, that prayer doesn't come easily to everyone. It can be a drudgery, a slog, even. But I've learned–and proven through hard, painful, repeated experience–that I need God, day by day and moment by moment, and that includes whenever I try to write.

So I pray. I pray before I write. I pray while I write. And then I pray after I write, that God will even further transform my offering through the work of godly publishers, editors, designers, artists, and so on. I pray, not to change God or others but to change me. I pray for wisdom to manage my time wisely, for discipline to apply my mind to my writing and my butt to the chair. I pray for my memory (at least until I forget). For some writing projects, I've assembled a prayer team to support my writing with their prayers, and I've tried to keep them up to date via email.

If you're at least as wise as me (which is not a high bar at all), you will make prayer your first writing assignment every day. Before you sharpen your pencil or turn on your computer, before you outline, before you jump into a writing exercise or research task, pray. Pray before you write, as you write, after you write. Pray for self-awareness, for focus, for inspiration, for protection. Pray to hear God clearly and to respond to him fully. Pray (as I often do) to write better than you are capable of writing.

That's why I offer this little volume of prayers for writers, assembling many of the prayers I've uttered over the years in the hope that others will use them to stoke the furnace of creativity, inspiration, and blessing in their own writing. If that happens, my own prayers will have been answered. And amplified. Amen.

Alpha and Omega

Alpha and Omega, First and Last, I pray:
be my first thought every morning,
and my last thought every night.

Claim my first allegiance,
my last full measure of devotion.

Take first place in my heart,
and rule over every last affection.

Make me first to serve,
last to seek credit.

Let me please you first,
and all others last, amen.

Word and Writer

In the beginning was the Word,
says your Word, Lord.

You identify yourself as Word, and Writer,
Speaker and Spoken.

You are the Source of all things.
Beginning.
Alpha.
First.

So let it be in me, and in my writing, Lord.
Be my first thought as I put pen to paper,
the Source and Supplier,
Word and Writer,
Speaker and Spoken.

Grant that I may pretend to no originality,
no creativity of my own,
but to be a thinker of your thoughts,
a writer of your words,
and herald of your good news
in all I write today, in Jesus' name, amen.

Words and Language

Thank you, God, for words and language,
for the mental, tactile, and often emotional pleasure of words on paper.

Thank you for the joy of a well-turned phrase,
the satisfaction of just the right word,
the beauty of an artful description,
a sonorous string of syllables,
or finely-tuned sentence.

Thank you for the honor of reflecting your image
in thinking and wording things into being,
bringing dead things (ideas, letters, pages) to life
and calling into existence things that do not exist (Romans 4:17).

Grant life to me today.
Grant life to my thoughts.
Grant life to my words.
Grant life to my writing,
in Jesus' name, amen.

Tools

Lord God, remind me today
that my primary tool is not the pen or paper,
Not the keyboard or computer,
Not a dictionary or thesaurus,
Not the Internet,
Not the alphabet,
Not my mind
Nor language itself...
But let me think and write in such a way
that your Spirit's voice is my greatest resource,
my greatest writing tool,
my guide,
in Jesus' name, amen.

Laziness

God, save me from laziness as a writer.
Save me from thinking my first draft is good enough.
Save me from settling for second best.
Save me from low standards,
pedestrian thoughts,
stale words,
and pat answers.

Grant me the grace to reread
and rewrite
with diligence and insight.

Grant me the stamina to edit and revise
with patience and perseverance.

Grant me the wisdom to be utterly unsatisfied
until every piece,
every page,
every paragraph and sentence
shines in such a way as to delight
both the reader and you,
in Jesus' name, amen.

Juggling

Lord, as I write today,
let your creativity flow through me,
along with your wisdom,
your insight,
your interest in people,
and your ability to love even those with desperate flaws.

Please give me focus beyond my abilities,
and productivity beyond my capacity.

You who can juggle galaxies and worlds,
and oversee the activity of angels and humans,
please help me to keep all the balls in the air:
setting, character, plot, subplot, flow, pace, etc.

Make me more like you than I can hope,
you who started my story,
and wove it into the great story
of you and your plans for this world,
this cosmos,
and every soul in it,
in Jesus' name, amen.

Instrument

God, from ancient days to modern times, you have chosen
human language to communicate with men and women;
you are a writer yourself, having written your commandments
in tablets of stone,
and your Word in my heart,
and my name in the Lamb's Book of Life.

You have also given me a love for the written word,
and have indebted me to the writings of many gifted men and
women.

So, while I am a feeble tool, I know that I am in the hands of a
mighty Master, and therefore I ask:
help me to stir up the gift of God that is within me;
help me to persevere when writing is hard,
when I am tired,
when my efforts are rejected;
help me to remember, when others seem to have a much
greater gift, an enviable talent, a natural ability,
that no one possesses the singular combination of my gift,
my personality, and my experience;
help me to submit to you all my talents and all my efforts,
never expecting the former to exceed the latter;
and help me strive to learn more of my craft at every
opportunity,
to develop my skills and fan the flame of my passions
so that I will not only be a writer,
but also an instrument of the Living God,
in Jesus' name, amen.

Verbs

I write today, Lord.
I will be using words, and some of them will be verbs.

Inspire them all, God, but especially the verbs.
Hover over them.
Speak them into existence.
Breathe into them the breath of life.

All my verbs come from you.
You are my "is," my "am," my "see," my "know."
You are my "laugh" and "cry," my "wake" and "sleep,"
"shiver" and "sweat," "think" and "speak,"
"jump" and "skip" and "dance" and "bounce."

There is not an action in my day,
a movement of my bones,
a breath in my breast
or a word on my tongue
that does not come from you.

Let it be consciously so in my writing today.
And at the end of my day, with the final word on the page,
pronounce it good, in Jesus' name, amen.

Fear

Save me from fear, Lord.
Give me courage to write;
make me "bold in our God" (1 Thessalonians 2:2 KJV) to write for you, whatever the obstacles or blockages the Enemy may throw in my way.

Save me from the fear of rejection;
let me write today for your approval first and foremost,
and if I receive it, let me be satisfied with it.

Save me from the fear of inadequacy;
remind me that "all my springs are in you" (Psalm 87:7 ESV),
and that you are wholly sufficient no matter how inadequate I may be...or feel.

Save me from the fear of failure.
I know, as Samuel Logan Brengle said, "Fear is a fruit of selfishness."
I confess my selfishness, my desire to amount to something.
Destroy that desire in me, and replace it with boldness and bravery.

Save me from the fear of success,
from all the "what ifs?" the future may hold.
As long as you are with me, I will not fear (Isaiah 41:10).

Save me also from the fear of criticism and ridicule.
Grant me willingness and boldness to think and work under your mighty hand, and to do it "as to the Lord, and not unto men" (Colossians 3:23 KJV), in Jesus' name, amen.

To Write Such Words

(based on stanzas from a hymn by Mary A. Lathbury)

You are the bread of life, dear Lord, to me,
your holy word the truth that rescues me.
Give me to eat and live with you above;
teach me to love your truth, for you are love.

O send your Spirit now, dear Lord, to me,
that he may touch my mind and set me free
to write such words of love, beauty, and grace,
that in them all who read may see your face.

A Prayer Before Writing

Lord God Adonai,
I am about to write.
I have nothing to say,
nothing to offer.
I am a poor writer,
and an even poorer Christian.
And yet I must try
to find words
that will bring into being
something that has never been before.
Help me, Lord.
Inspire me.
Empower me.
Flow through me.
Grant that I may write
better than I can write,
and thus know that
all the honor and glory and thanks
belong to you,
in Jesus' name, amen.

Against the Blank Page

Almighty God, I sit and stare,
a blank white screen
before me where
soon should be seen
the things I want to write.

It's hard sometimes
to make a start
to fashion lines
to practice art
with what I want to write.

Help me rely on you
to move my mind
to push me through
until I find
the words I want to write.

On Starting a New Project

Abba, Father,
thank you for the work you have given me to do,
for what I am about to write.
I begin in fear and trembling,
not at all sure that I can start well, let alone finish well.
But your grace is sufficient for me,
in writing as in all of life,
for your strength is made perfect in my weakness.
Take my weakness, all of it.
I give it to you.
Take my strength, what little I have.
Take my mind, my voice, my fingers, my keyboard,
my thought processes and nerve impulses
and combine them all to produce something of value
for those who will someday read what I am about to write.
Let your sanctified creativity flow through me,
body and soul,
and let me remember at day's end
to give you thanks for every mercy and grace I experience
in the writing process,
in Jesus' name, amen.

Self Doubt

Who am I, Lord,
that I think I can write,
that I have anything to say,
that I can speak sometimes for you?
I have a middling brain, at best,
and some education,
but the longer I live, the less I know, it seems.
I can be lazy, thick-headed, shortsighted, and careless.
There are so many others
who seem so much brighter and bolder,
so much more inspired and insightful than I think I can ever be.
Sure, Moses felt inadequate, too.
And Jeremiah.
Paul, too.
I easily forget that they weren't all that confident and serene
when you called them,
or even as you were using them.
But you used them.
So maybe you can do something with me.
Help me to trust that possibility,
and to write better than I think I can,
in Jesus' name, amen.

Rejection

Lord Jesus,
I guess if anyone knows how rejection feels, you do.
I know it's a part of being a writer,
hearing "not right for us"
and "not right for our audience"
and "not a good time"
or, worse, nothing at all.
Sometimes it seems so few and far between acceptances.
I know, I know:
You set your face like a flint
even when you knew what lay ahead.
So, okay, I'm not trudging to Calvary.
I'm not carrying a cross.
I'm learning to do better,
to write to the reader's need,
to study the editor's requirements,
to hone my craft and trust your timing.
Help me to start again tomorrow,
and the day after, and so on,
while learning to find my acceptance and my worth in you.
Amen.

A Writer's Psalm 23

Lord, you are my inspiration; I don't take that for granted.

You send me to my writing spot;
You lead me to the right word,
You refresh my soul along with my prose.
You guide me along the right paths
for the sake of your name and your message.

Even though I walk
through dark valleys of indecision and frustration,
I will not fear, for you are with me;
your Word and your presence, they comfort me.

I will keep believing that you will prepare a book table for me,
of volumes you have inspired and shepherded all the way
through publication.

I rely on your sweet anointing;
my cup overflows,
and your goodness and love will follow me
all the days of my writing life,
and I will dwell in your presence until I hear your "well done,"
amen.

Nouns

I use too many adjectives
and adverbs as I write;
I want the lift a good noun gives
to help a phrase take flight,
like dandelion, balustrade,
and cricket, poppy, trough,
and foghorn, meadow, cannonade,
assassin, scythe, and toff,
and more, I pray, from You who gave
each item, object, thing,
and every single noun I have
to make my writing sing.

Jealousy

Lord, I confess that I am a jealous writer,
jealous of this one's sales figures,
that one's income,
this other one's ideas,
his creativity
and her marketing skills
and yet another's craftsmanship.
I know that this is a fallen world,
but I often feel (and act) more fallen than the rest.
At least that's something I can claim
and not be jealous of in another.

My Simple Prayer Today

Gracious Lord,
my prayer for my writing
is for my writing to be my prayer.
Amen.

I Need You

(based on verses by Annie S. Hawks and refrain by Robert Lowry)

I need you every hour, most gracious Lord;
No tender voice like yours can peace afford.

I need you, oh, I need you;
Every hour I need you;
Oh, bless me now, my Savior,
I come to you.

I need you every hour, I need your presence here,
My words resound with power whenever you are near.

I need you every hour, that all I write may be
A fitting sacrifice, an offering from me.

Technology

Abba, my Father,
thank you for technology.
Thank you for the inventions and discoveries
that enrich my life
though they also complicate it at times.

Thank you for cell phones and computers,
television and radio;
for the internet,
remote controls,
eBooks,
iPads,
and applications,
word processing,
email,
scanning,
digital photography,
pdfs,
Skype
Facebook
Twitter
and blogs.

Thank you for text messaging
and music apps
and syncing calendars
and address books
and alarms and notifications
and financial software
and presentation software
and desktop publishing software
and so much more.

Thank you, Lord,
for the ability to download an eBook in seconds,
send a message around the world in a moment,
pay a bill,
answer a question,
save a coupon,
make a reservation,
and listen to music
in ways that were impossible just a short time ago.

Thank you for technology,
for the helpful purposes it serves,
even as I pray for you to frustrate
the evil ways it can also be used,
in Jesus' name, amen.

Research

God, thank you for one of the most fun parts of being a writer: Research.

Thank you for the alluring rabbit trails
and multiple (even conflicting) sources
and fascinating discoveries
that make research so enjoyable.

Thank you for the availability of information
in libraries, from experts, in publications, and books.

Thank you for the thrill of tracing a quote or fact
or some other detail
backward through layers of secondary sources
to find the origin,
even when it necessitates a change of plan.

Thank you for the blessings and dangers
of living and writing
and researching
in the Information Age,
in Jesus' name, amen.

A Short Invocation Before Writing

O for a muse of fire
that would ascend
the brightest heaven of invention
(Henry V, Prologue, 1).

Against Stupid Mistakes

Lord, I hate when I do that–
when I make stupid writing mistakes,
usually because I'm too lazy to outline,
too careless in research,
or too rushed to revise,
or all three!

Please save me from my own stupid mistakes.
Make me more careful and conscientious.
Help me to write wisely and well.
Purge me of procrastination and presumption.
Give me grace to keep me learning, striving,
and constantly improving,
in Jesus' name, amen.

Twelve Bible Prayers for My Writing

Father God, let my heart be stirred today by a noble theme and make my tongue, mind, heart, pen, and keyboard that of a skillful writer (Psalm 45:1).

Help me to do as you told the prophet: write down what you show me, and make it clear "so that the message will be easy to read" (Habakkuk 2:2 ERV).

Grant that as I "grow in the grace and knowledge of our Lord and Savior Jesus Christ" (2 Peter 3:18), my effectiveness as a writer may also develop and grow.

Grant also that as I live a life of love, through the Spirit who dwells in me (Ephesians 5:2, Galatians 5:22), my writing may always be motivated by the love of God.

Let integrity and honesty always characterize my efforts at writing and publishing (Psalm 25:21).

Lord, your Word is more precious than gold, than much pure gold, and sweeter than honey, than honey from the honeycomb (Psalm 19:10). Help me to handle it wisely and responsibly, as a worker who does not need to be ashamed (2 Timothy 2:15).

Keep me always aware that your Spirit's voice is my greatest resource, my greatest writing tool, and my guide (Acts 4:31).

Let my work as a writer shine so as to reflect the fact that I am your workmanship, created in Christ Jesus to do good works (Ephesians 2:10).

Give me focus today beyond my ability, creativity beyond my facility, and productivity beyond my capacity (inspired by 1 Thessalonians 1:3).

Purge me of procrastination and presumption. Make me careful and conscientious (1 Samuel 25:28; James 3:2).

Make me a scribe who has been trained for the kingdom of heaven, who brings out of my treasure what is new and what is old (Matthew 13:52).

And grant that I may reach the end of this writing day in awed gratitude for your presence in my life and in my work (Psalm 89:15).

Amen.

Plagiarism

Lord, I don't like it
when others commandeer or confiscate my words
and pass them off as their own,
so please let me never be guilty,
in even the smallest detail,
of doing to others
what I don't want done to me,
in Jesus' name, amen.

For Bible Translations

Abba, thank you for the hundreds
of Bible translations that are available to me,
and for their forerunners throughout history,
who have made
your precious Word
understandable and accessible, often at great personal cost.

Thank you for of the 72 Jewish elders recruited by Ptolemy II
who translated the Old Testament from Hebrew into Greek.

Thank you for William Tyndale,
who gave his life to "Write down the revelation and make it plain" (Habakkuk 2:2).

Thank you for the 47 scholars who transformed the Textus Receptus into the beauty and majesty of the King James Version.

Thank you for Moffatt and Phillips,
for Ken Taylor and Eugene Peterson,
for the 32 scholars who gave us the NASB,
and the more than 100 scholars who produced the NIV.

Thank you for the efforts of more than 90 scholars
that went into the New Living Translation,
and that of the scores of scholars and advisors
who produced the English Standard Version.

May my appreciation and obedience to your Word
honor their efforts,
and yours in inspiring them.

May my life translate Scripture
into a language those around me can read,
in Jesus' name, amen.

Must I Kill All My Little Darlings?

They are waiting for me, all my little darlings.
I've labored over them as if in the pangs of childbirth.
I have nurtured them,
weighed and coddled them,
smiled at them and played with them.
They have grown and multiplied,
and though at times they are recalcitrant, I have loved them.

How many must go? Which ones are weak, superfluous,
misplaced, unclear, redundant?

You know, Lord.
I approach them now as a gardener, not a butcher.
But it still hurts.
Give me clarity, give me fortitude.
Make me merciless, make me wise.
Supply boldness, supply discretion.
And in your kindness and creativity,
let every syllable that is trimmed, every phrase that is
straightened,
be obedience to you,
a credit to me,
and a blessing to the reader,
in Jesus' name, amen.

Proclaiming Good Tidings

(based on 1 Chronicles 16:23-24)

I write today for you, Lord;
Let me proclaim good tidings of your salvation in every word,
and tell of your glory in every line,
your wonderful deeds to all who will read.

Save Me from Success

Father, save me from success.
From wealth. Awards. Fame. Status.
Save me from a mindset that measures my worth by this world's standards.
Save me from becoming enamored with my own words, ideas or ingenuity.
Save me from overreaching,
from outrunning your pace, and your plans for me.
Save me from trusting in myself,
from becoming smug or self-satisfied,
from unhealthy expectations and harmful comforts.

Let nothing come too easily
or more quickly to me
than your wisdom dictates.

Save my writing from becoming pedestrian,
my habits from becoming staid,
my prayers from going stale,
and my life from being predictable.

As you have done so far
please do for the rest of my journey:
Let me work hard for every achievement
and acknowledge you in every blessing,
in Jesus' name, amen.

A Prayer for My Readers

What a privilege is mine
to write
and to publish.
What an honor
that people around the world
and down through the years
will be able to read these words
I write today.

I pray for every one of my readers, Lord:
Those who will seek out my words,
those who will receive them from a friend,
those who will stumble upon them,
those who will read them only because
there's nothing else at hand.
Let each of them find you in what I write.
Let every one be drawn closer to you by these words.
Let the clarity and quality of my work today
pay eternal dividends
and glorify you
exceeding abundantly above I can imagine or dream,
in Jesus' name, amen.

A Prayer Before Pressing "Send"

I think it's ready, Lord.
I've written, rewritten, edited, and proofread.
It's been critiqued and revised yet again.
I hover my cursor over "Send."
I tremble...with trepidation...and excitement.
And faith. Right? Maybe faith.
Maybe, since I've trusted you
and believed that you've been guiding me in the creative process,
I can keep believing that you will guide the process of submission.
Maybe.
I'm tempted to wait. Maybe look it over again, before sending.
But I've done that, repeatedly.
So.
Lord, hear my prayer.
Bless it in the sending as I hope you have in the writing.

Here goes...

A Writer's Thanks

Gracious Lord,
thank you for the joy of writing.
For the honor of being published.
For the blessing of being used.
The miracle of being paid.
The wonder of being read.
The blessing of my words being translated
and traveling around the world.
Amen.

A Writer's Questions

Lord, you know writers.
You know us forward and backward, in and out.
You know all the questions we ask,
all the uncertainties over which we labor.
When can I call myself a writer?
Why are my submissions rejected?
When will I be published?
Why does it take so long?
What am I doing wrong?
When can I say I'm an author?
Why isn't my manuscript where I thought I put it?

So many questions.
For today, though, help me to put them aside (once I find that manuscript)
and focus fully on you
and hear clearly what you seem to be saying to me...
and what you might want to say through my writing.

Quiet the questions, please.
Let me hear your still, small voice over my insecurities,
In Jesus' name, amen.

Against Clichés, Platitudes, Qualifiers, Jargon, and Overdone Words

Living Word, help me in my writing, to eschew all:

Cliches, even when they're biblical,
such as "white as snow" and "writing on the wall."

And platitudes
such as "Don't sweat the small stuff" or "God helps those who help themselves."

As well as qualifiers
such as rather, very, pretty, and little.

Or jargon, especially Christianese terms
such as "blood-washed" and "get on our faces."

Along with overdone words,
including "epic," "awesome," "impacted, or "downsized."

And save me also from mixed metaphors
that make editors scream like banshees until the cows come home.

Amen.

To Write Like Me

It's tempting, Lord,
to ask for the grace
of being able to write
like Annie Dillard
or Frederick Buechner
Eugene Peterson,
or Wendell Berry.
Or even,
throwing caution to the wind,
like Paul
or John
or Isaiah
or David.
But I will ask instead,
humbly but wholeheartedly:
Please let me write
like me,
the best me of all possible mes,
in Jesus' name, amen.

Word of God, Speak

Word of God, speak.
Awake my senses.
Inspire my thoughts.
Supply my words.

I confess that I have poured forth speech
out of the emptiness and vagrancy of my own soul.
I have settled for my words
rather than listening and waiting for your words.
Not today.

Word of God, speak.
Let my conscious and unconscious thoughts be inspired
repetition of your thoughts.
Let my words flow from your mind and your hand.
Choose them and mold them
with the reader in mind,
the soul whom you would move and touch and change
by the words I write today.

Come, Word of God. Speak,
in Jesus' name, amen.

A Writer's Confession

Lord God Almighty, I confess that I have sinned against you through my own fault, in thought and word and deed, by what I have done and by what I have left undone.

I confess that I have too often trusted my own strength instead of relying on yours;
I have let my puny ability suffice when I could have and should have laid hold of your ready power.

I confess that I have chased after mammon, and written for mere money,
instead of seeking first your kingdom and your glory, and writing to please you.

I confess that I have been jealous of other writers and their success,
and have been ungrateful for all the kindness you have shown me.

I confess that I have taken shortcuts in my writing
and have been lazy in the hard work of planning and researching,
of editing and rewriting,
of reviewing and proofreading.

I confess that I have neglected prayer,
as if my activity is more important than yours in my writing.

I confess that I have chosen leisure over discipline,
speed over craft,
and my voice instead of your voice.

Thank you for the assurance of your forgiveness through my Lord, Jesus Christ.

Please cleanse me from sin and help me to write for you, in holiness and righteousness all my days,
in Jesus' name, amen.

Pink Slip Prayer

Father, thank you
for the publisher that said "no, thank you" today.

I had high hopes for that one.
I really thought it would be a yes.
But you know best, and I trust your wisdom and love,
even when it hurts.

Maybe you have something else planned.
Something better.
Or maybe you're teaching me something.
I hope it's the "something better" option.

I Have to Laugh

I have to laugh, Lord.

You know how I value security–especially the financial kind–
and must stretch to trust you (instead of myself)
to provide for my family's needs.

You know that I like predictability
and struggle to trust you when things change.

You know how personally I take rejection,
and must strive for your approval instead of man's.

So you made me a writer.
I have to laugh,
or I just might cry.

Ingenuity

Lord, save me from trusting
in myself,
in my ideas,
in my ingenuity.

Give me the gift of faith in you,
your ideas,
your ingenuity,
your voice,
your power,
your words, in Jesus' name, amen.

Need

Good God, my Father,
I will need you today.
I always need you, in all I do,
but I confess I am not always aware of it.
But I am keenly aware of it today.
I need your energy and inspiration as I write.
I need your focus and clarity,
your moment-by-moment deliverance from distraction.
I need your encouragement and empowerment.
I need, most of all, the sweet fragrance of your presence,
the constant assurance of your favor,
and the realization of your creativity and love and truth
flowing through me,
to the glory of your name and the blessing of my readers.

Please grant
that I may reach the end of this writing day
in awed gratitude for your presence in my life,
and your provision in my work,
in Jesus' name, amen.

Through

Lord, please let your thoughts flow
through my thoughts,
through my heart,
through the tips of my fingers,
through my keyboard,
through my computer,
through my manuscript,
through my edits,
through my editor's edits,
through the publishing process,
through the marketing process,
into my readers' minds
and to their hearts,
in Jesus' name, amen.

Far From Done

Father God, thank you for giving me some of the skills and traits a writer needs,
though I know you're far from done with me.

Please make me more observant, both in the moment of an experience and as I reflect on such moments. Cause me to see more than is my wont, to mark details, patterns, and anomalies. Expand and intensify my vision and augment it with a sharp and enduring recall.

Please make me more insightful. Help me to see not merely with, but through, the eye.
Inspire me not only to see but to interpret, unravel, understand. Prompt me to recognize the important, the good, the bad, and the ugly in all I observe. Help me, as so many fine writers do, to make electrifying connections between seemingly unrelated things for myself and for my readers.

Please make me more expressive in thought and in word. Grant me virtuosity in conveying thoughts and ideas. Make me the Miles Davis of the written word. The Vincent Van Gogh. The Nadia Comăneci.

Please make me more articulate. Fluent. Clear. Precise. Teach me to use the right word, just so. Help me to not only say something worth saying, but to say it with such clarity that there can be no misunderstanding.

All this I ask, in Jesus' name, amen.

A Writer's Haiku

My roots seem shallow,
My branches bare. Prune, water,
shine, and bring forth fruit.

A Writer's Senryu

Here I am, alone
But not alone; you are here.
Speak in the silence.

Only Speak the Word

"Only speak the word," the centurion said to you, Jesus.
It is my prayer, too.

Only speak the word: and I will write what you say to write.
Only speak the word: and I will wait.
Only speak the word: and I will stop.
Only speak the word: and I will start again.
Only speak the word: and I will bow in prayer.
Only speak the word: and I will whisper.
Only speak the word: and I will shout.
Only speak the word: and I will tell a story.
Only speak the word: and I will shut my mouth.
Only speak the word: and I will search the Scriptures.
Only speak the word: and I will take a walk.
Only speak the word: and I will throw caution to the wind.
Only speak the word: and I will answer.
Amen.

I Speak to the Mountains

Jesus, you said if I have faith as small as a mustard seed, I could say to a mountain, "Move from here to there," and it would move (Matthew 17:20).

So I will.
I speak to the mountain of tasks that await me this day; let it be accomplished.
I speak to the mountain of self-doubt that tells me I can't write; let it be gone.
I speak to the mountain of weariness that tempts me to loaf; let it be removed.
I speak to the mountain of distractions that allure me away from my desk; let it be still.
I speak to the mountain of confusion that keeps me from seeing things clearly; be dispelled.
I speak to the mountain of panic that makes me despair of meeting my deadline; be gone.
I speak to the mountain of words I have yet to write; be written.
I speak to the mountain of things I have yet to learn; be done.
I speak to the mountain of weakness that tempts me to settle for less than the best I have to give; be vanquished,
in Jesus' name, amen.

For a Manuscript Just Sent

Lord God, you turned back the sun ten degrees on the sundial
in answer to your servant Hezekiah's prayers.
You reminded your prophet Jeremiah,
"Is anything too hard for me?"
So I pray, God-for-whom-nothing-is-hard,
make my just-submitted manuscript better than I made it.
Since I must now abandon it into another's hands,
I ask you not to abandon it,
but to make any and every change in it
that I was too unhearing, dull, or distracted to make.
Be my Editor before any other,
in Jesus' name, amen.

Double Portion Prayer

Gracious God, who inspired faulty and feeble men in times past to write for the purpose of changing lives, please let some of that spirit–a double portion, even, as I am more faulty and feeble than they–rest on me as a writer.

Grant me the productivity of Moses, who though he lived in an age before paper or press is credited with "the books of Moses," revered as Torah by one generation after another.

Grant me David's lyricism and imagery evident in line after line of psalm after psalm, from "The LORD is my shepherd" (Psalm 23:1) to "He who dwells in the secret place of the Most High shall abide under the shadow of the Almighty." (Psalm 91:1 KJV)

Grant me Isaiah's facility with word and phrase, he who wrote "Wonderful, Counselor, Mighty God, Everlasting Father, Prince of Peace," (Isaiah 9:6) and "They that wait upon the LORD shall renew their strength; they shall mount up with wings as eagles; they shall run and not grow weary, they shall walk and not faint." (Isaiah 40:8 KJV)

Grant me Solomon's wisdom, Ezekiel's vision, Jeremiah's compulsion, and Daniel's spine.

Grant me Hosea's courage in telling my story, and in obeying and reflecting you in its every twist and turn.

Grant me the Gospel writers' recall. Luke's accuracy. Paul's intensity. James's practicality.

And grant, please, whenever my end approaches, whatever my final book or sentence may be, a finish like that of your servant John.

All this I am so bold to ask only through the merit of my Savior, Lord, and King, in whose name I ask it, amen.

A Writer's Lament

(loosely based on Psalm 6:2-10)

Have mercy on me, Lord, for I am so weary.
Heal me, Lord, for my heart is hurting.
This writer's soul is in deep anguish.
How long, Lord, how long?
How much rejection must I endure?
How many revisions?

Come, Lord, and deliver me;
I know you love me, please show it in my writing.
I do my best to proclaim your name.
But how will people ever read my words?
I'm worn out from asking.
I've cried and cried over these pages.
I've given myself headaches from staring at a screen.
I've read books and attended conferences.

Lord, listen to my weeping.
Hear my cry for mercy;
accept my prayer.
Relieve my sadness
and send me some encouragement, some sign of your favor,
Amen.

A Prayer Before Reading

Father God, as I sit down to read this book,
I ask you for help.
By your grace,
overcome my weariness,
dullness,
lack of focus,
and anything else that would hinder my understanding.
Help me to grasp what the author is saying,
weigh it wisely,
and by it come to a new place of understanding and experience–
one that meets your approval and increases my usefulness as your servant,
in Jesus' name, amen.

The Tools of My Trade

Lord, these words from *The Message* paraphrase seem fitting today:

The tools of our trade aren't for marketing or manipulation, but they are for demolishing [a] massively corrupt culture. We use our powerful God-tools for smashing warped philosophies, tearing down barriers erected against the truth of God, fitting every loose thought and emotion and impulse into the structure of life shaped by Christ. Our tools are ready at hand for clearing the ground of every obstruction and building lives of obedience into maturity (2 Corinthians 10:4-6 *The Message*).

Help me, please, to use God-tools as I write. Help me to fit every loose thought, emotion, and impulse into the structure of a life shaped by Christ. Clear every obstruction and help me to write not only with my thoughts, fingers, and words, but also and especially with my life, in Jesus' name, amen.

A Writer's Dream

Lord, you showed Jacob a stairway to heaven,
and spoke to Solomon in his dreams.
You gave to Joseph and Daniel
insight into the meaning of dreams,
and gave your servant Peter a transforming vision.

God of dreams and visions,
please condescend to me in my sleep,
and inspire my writing even as I sleep.
Speak to me in the night watches,
whisper in my ear,
and make me a better writer
while I rest in your arms,
in Jesus' name, amen.

A Prayer from Adoniram Judson

(based on words ascribed to Adoniram Judson, from the book, *Splendor of God,* by Honore Willsie Morrow (New York: A. L. Burt & Company, 1929), p. 370)

Good God, grant that I may kneel down before you and with the last leaf in my hand, imploring your forgiveness for all the sins which have polluted my labors and your aid in future efforts to remove the errors and imperfections which necessarily cleave to my work, commend my work to your mercy and grace. I have dedicated it all to your glory. May you transform my faulty words into your own inspired words, and make them a grand instrument for the blessing of others and the means of filling the whole world with songs of praise to you. Amen.

A Prayer for My Book

Abba, Father, Author of all good things,
my book will be coming out soon.
But then, you already knew that.
In fact, you already know who will see it,
who will buy it,
who will read it,
who will recommend it to others.
Multiply that company, Lord.
Prepare each of those souls for the entrance of your Word.
Oversee the timing of the book's release and promotion with them in mind.

Inspire me with new and value-added ways to announce and promote the book.
Bless the efforts of influencers and early readers to spread the word.
Grant that reader enthusiasm and word-of-mouth may dwarf all other promotional efforts.
Create a groundswell of excitement and "buzz."
Place it prominently on blogs and social media
and best seller lists.
Make it an immediate and enduring blessing to tens–even hundreds–of thousands of souls.
Use its success to support my coming writing and ministry efforts, and to make possible greater and bolder efforts for its publisher in the future.

Let the words of my mind and the publication of my thoughts
be acceptable in your sight, O Lord, my strength and my redeemer.
Amen.

Save From Excuse-Making

Lord God,
I remember that Samuel Logan Brengle wrote in a sick bed,
and Ken Taylor wrote on a train;
Dietrich Bonhoeffer wrote in prison,
the Apostle Paul while chained to a guard.
Let the same Spirit who inspired those men
save me from excuse-making,
and energize my writing,
wherever I am,
in whatever circumstance,
in Jesus' name, amen.

A Prayer to Begin the Workday

(from a hymn by Charles Wesley)

Summoned my labor to renew,
And glad to act my part,
Lord, in Thy name my work I do,
And with a single heart.

End of my every action Thou,
In all things Thee I see;
Accept my offered labor now.
I do it unto Thee.

In Your Time

Heavenly Father,
you make everything beautiful in your time (Ecclesiastes 3:11).

I submit to your timing.
I await your timing.
I desire what you will,
as you will,
when you will.

That goes for my writing, too.

I long to touch lives with my words...in your time.
I want to write passionately, effectively, impactfully...in your time.
I yearn to think and communicate clearly and sharply...in your time.
I pray to craft artful, beautiful words, sentences, and passages... in your time.
I ask for publication, for contracts, for endorsements, for readers, and for life-changing influence...in your time,
in Jesus' name, amen.

Creation and Imitation

Lord God, beautiful Creator,
I have yet to create anything.

From mud pies to masterpieces,
everything I have formed or fashioned
has been a simple, sometimes crude, rearrangement
of your mighty works.

I have ever and always used the raw materials you provide
to make something that seemed new
but was in reality an imitation of you,
of your words, of your wonders.

Sometimes, I confess,
I have cravenly tried to imitate
others who imitate you:
poets, prophets, and preachers,
artists and musicians,
whose gifts for reflecting your beauty and imagination
inspire awe and envy in me.

But they are imitators, too.
So save me, Lord, from imitating other imitators.
Grant that I may always–
and with increasing artistry–
imitate only you,
the sole Creator,
the true Innovator,
the only Originator of all beauty and creativity,
in Jesus' name, amen.

Guide Me

(adapted from a hymn by William Williams)

Guide me, O thou great Jehovah,
as I write with feeble hand.
I am weak, but thou art mighty;
hold me with thy powerful hand.
Bread of heaven, bread of heaven,
feed me till I want no more.

Open now the crystal fountain,
whence the streams of inspiration flow;
let the fire and cloudy pillar
light the way you'd have me go.
Strong deliverer, strong deliverer,
be thou still my strength and shield.

When I hit the wall in writing,
all my anxious fears forfend;
keep me thinking, keep me writing,
till I reach the happy end.
Songs of praises, songs of praises,
I will ever give to thee.

Forgive My Little Efforts

Father God Almighty,
you inspired Moses, Samuel, and others
to write when their best tools
were papyrus and parchment,
reed styli and ink made from crushed berries and plants.

For millennia,
your servants have recorded
stirring and soaring works
in caves and cells,
dusty rooms and mud huts,
by lamplight and candlelight.

So many have written so well
in such circumstances
as to shame my little efforts
and shoddy craftsmanship.

So forgive me, Lord,
when I let tiny obstacles
and minor inconveniences
compromise my praying and writing.
Forgive all those times when I could do better
and make them less and less frequent
until they sink forever beneath the waves of creativity
imagination,
and productivity,
in Jesus' name, amen.

Signature

Woodworker, builder, craftsman in stone,
in your shop by the smith's,
in the door of your home,
with plumbline to measure, plane to make smooth,
midst curlings and shavings of sweet-scented wood,
knotted and grained, olivewood, oak,
with bow-drill and bit, wood mallet, awl,
mold table and chair, threshing-board, yoke,
winnowing fork, plow, a child's handhewn toy.

Sweat-streamed, leather-wrapped,
with ax and adz in hand,
you chisel and chip,
cut, hammer, scrape, grind,
file and sand, polish, and buff,
till your craftsmanship shines
in the figure you form.

Carpenter, Artist, sharpen your tools,
Carve your signature in me.

In What I Am Writing Now

Lord God,
in your almighty power and eternal purpose,
let all that I am
enjoying now,
enduring now,
thinking now,
feeling now,
hearing now,
reading now,
observing now,
absorbing now,
experiencing now,
combine and coalesce
in what I am writing now
so as to bear fruit for your good purposes
in the hearts and minds of many,
in Jesus' name, amen.

You Wrote Me

Great Author of my life, you conceived,
drafted, revised, edited me.
You wrote me when no one else
knew or cared for my soul.
Now publish me. Let
those who read be
changed like
me.

A Writer's Psalm 61

Hear my cry, God;
Please listen to my prayer.
From my writing desk I call to you,
I call as my heart grows faint;
lead me to the rock that is higher than I.

For you have been my refuge,
a strong tower against every foe.

I long to write for you
To write well-chosen words that please you and bless others.

For you, God, look into my heart;
you see every desire...and all of my shortcomings.
Bless my thoughts and words.
Speak to me and through me.

Be enthroned in every sentence I write.
Let your love and faithfulness shine through each paragraph and page.

Let my writing sing your praise
and fulfill your will, not mine. Amen.

Speak to Me

Please speak to me in my writing today, Lord.
Please enlighten me that I may enlighten others.
Inspire me that I may inspire those who read.
Fill me that I may write from a fulness of spirit.
Focus me that I may communicate clearly and well,
in Jesus' name, amen.

Hurry

Teach me, Lord, that hurry is not my friend.
Give me patience and perseverance in my writing life.

Save me from rushing,
from running ahead,
taking shortcuts and side trips
rather than waiting on you,
putting in the time,
thinking carefully and thoroughly,
and writing from a place and posture of alert, expectant composure,
in Jesus' name, amen.

Deadlines

Thank you, Lord, for the deadlines
that give structure
and impetus
to my writing life.

Help me to meet every one,
and to beat them often enough
as to be a blessing to the editors and publishers
who are foolish enough or kind enough
to give me work,
in Jesus' name, amen.

Prayer from a Line of Emerson

Lord God,
Emerson said, "The writer is an explorer.
Every step is an advance into new land."[1]

As I embark on today's writing adventure,
guard my steps.
Shine your light on my path.
Whisper in my ear which way to go.
And help me to listen attentively
rather than offer the sacrifice of fools,
who don't even know that they have wandered away from wisdom (Ecclesiastes 5:1),
in Jesus' name, amen.

[1]Ralph Waldo Emerson, *The Journals of Ralph Waldo Emerson,* Robert N. Linscott, ed. (New York: Random House, 1960), 452.

A Writer's Hymn

(from a hymn by Francis Ridley Havergal)

Take my life, and let it be consecrated, Lord, to Thee.
Take my moments and my days; let them flow in ceaseless praise.
Take my hands, and let them move at the impulse of Thy love.
Take my intellect, and use every power as Thou shalt choose.

Take my keyboard, and my screen; my desk and office chair,
My pages, sentences, and words, my flittings here and there,
My focus and my flow, my pacings up and down,
My insecurities and fears, my grins, my groans, my frowns.

Let every bit be used by you, the good, the bad, and ugly too.
Make me better than I know to be, by being yours while being me,
Let every word I type be true by coming first and most from you.
Suggest, revise, inform, inspire, and take my writing higher and higher.

Take my fingertips, let them be filled with messages from Thee.
Take my will, and make it Thine; it shall be no longer mine.
Take my heart, it is Thine own; it shall be Thy royal throne.
Take my love, my Lord, I pour at Thy feet its treasure store.

Another Writer's Hymn

(from a hymn by William Freeman Lloyd)

My times are in your hand;
my God, I wish them there;
my life, my soul, my words, I leave
entirely to your care.

My times are in your hand,
whatever I may do;
to write, to publish, soon or late,
as may seem best to you.

My times are in your hand;
I need not rush or fear;
I know your hand will never cause
your child a needless tear.

My times are in your hand;
I'll wait and trust your plan,
and know my writing hopes and dreams
are safely in your hands.

Words Fitly Written

Lord,
grant that I may produce today
words fitly written,
that shine
like apples of gold
in settings of silver,
in Jesus' name, amen.

Until the Floodgates Open

Lord, I'm behind.
I have a deadline, a goal,
and I have fallen behind.
I will keep working,
inspiration or no inspiration.
I will keep plodding,
and try not to stress.
I will do my best
to let you do all the planning and plotting
while I simply follow along,
step by step,
word by word,
line by line,
page by painstaking page,
until the momentum shifts,
the floodgates open,
and words flow like streams in April,
amen.

Amanuensis

Lord, make me your amanuensis.
Your scribe. Your secretary.
Think aloud to me,
slowly and simply enough
that I can transcribe the things you want to say
to me,
through me.
Tune the ears of my heart,
train my fingers to flow,
my muscles to move,
at the slightest inflection of your voice,
the tiniest trace of meaning
from your mind.
Amen.

Fruit

Holy Spirit,
cultivate and proliferate your fruit in my writing.

Let love permeate my words.
Help me experience joy in the writing,
and let my readers experience joy in reading.
Use my writing to spread shalom.
Give me patience in the writing.
Let goodness characterize what I write,
and gentleness how I write it.
Make and keep me faithful to you, to the publisher, and to the reader from beginning to end,
and let God-given self-control guide my every thought,
impulse, and decision as I write, revise, edit, and review,
in Jesus' name, amen.

Transform

Lord Jesus,
you turned a meager lunch into a banquet for thousands,
a common lake trout into an ATM,
a brash fisherman into a water-walker,
a skeptical Thomas into a staunch devotee,
and a grisly death into death's defeat.

Please turn my faulty thoughts and flailing words
into something worth reading.
Amen.

Mantle

Lord, Elisha asked for a double portion of Elijah's spirit, the eldest son's inheritance, to rest upon him. And it was given to him.

I ask, too, for the mantle of a prophet,
for a generous inheritance as a writer:
for insight like Leonard Sweet,
for the pastorly heart and mind of Eugene Peterson,
for creativity like Calvin Miller,
the energy of Josh McDowell,
sensitivity of Brennan Manning,
lyricism of Wendell Berry,
productivity of Jerry Jenkins,
and influence of N. T. Wright.

I feel silly and arrogant praying such a prayer, but I do so on the basis of James 4:2, in full awareness of my own unworthiness and your surpassing worth and willingness to answer prayer, in Jesus' name, amen.

But Your Own

(based on the first verse of a hymn by William How)

I give you but your own,
What writing I may do;
All I have is yours alone,
A trust that comes from you.

For Writing Tools

For fountain pens and India ink,
Legal pads and time to think,
Olivetti, Underwood, Selectric,
Typewriters both manual and electric,
Typing paper, carbon paper,
Correction ribbon and Liquid Paper,
Dictionaries and thesauri,
Keyboards, touchpads, countless styli,
Strunk and White and Zinsser, too,
Staples, tape, and Elmer's Glue,
Desktops, laptops, iPads, printers,
Modems, faxes, scanners, shredders,
Voice recording and dictation,
Chairs for work and relaxation,
Templates, shortcuts, tips and tricks,
Cross pens, Sheaffers, Pilots, Bics,
For all the tools that have played their part,
Flow thanks from this poor writer's heart.

Guide My Reading

God,
in your infinite wisdom,
please guide my reading
so as to inspire
and inform
what you want me to think,
what you want me to notice,
what you want me to remember,
what you want me to write,
and what you want me to quote,
in Jesus' name,
amen.

For Things Important to a Writer

Abba, Father, Lord God,
thank you that I can type so fast,
that the internet makes research relatively easy (if dangerous),
that I can work at home or in a coffee shop.

Thank you that I can send manuscripts and galleys via email,
that I can quickly search a document,
that I can access, order, and download books online.

Thank you that I can choose between screen and paper,
digital or analog, old ways and new ways.

Thank you for the quiet of my home office,
and for the vast choices of music I can tap into
to accompany and enliven my writing hours.

Thank you for the ability to scan and print,
to edit in hard copy or onscreen, to sit or stand as I write.

Thank you for the "Do Not Disturb" function on my phone,
for the "Reminders" I can set,
and for the layers of timed online backups,
in Jesus' name, amen.

Godstorm

Lord,
I could sit down and brainstorm ideas
for something fun, interesting, worthwhile–maybe even
profitable–
to write.

But I would much rather write Godstormed ideas.
Would you please send a storm
of inspiration
to my little brain?

Thank you.
Amen.

My Eyes Are On You

Lord, my eyes are on you.
I trust you for my writing,
for all my hopes, plans, and dreams.
I trust you in the macro AND in the micro,
in the giving and taking,
and in the timing as well.

I seek you,
and your will, in Jesus' name, amen.

A Writer's Education

Teach me your ways, Lord.
Teach me your Word.
Teach me your wit.
Teach me your winsomeness.
Teach me your wiles.
Teach me your will.
Teach me your wealth of creativity,
resources,
variety,
and beauty.
Teach me your wonders,
in Jesus' name, amen.

A Writer's Evening Prayer

(based on a hymn by C. Maud Battersby)

If I have failed to heed your voice today,
If I have driven any of your thoughts away,
If I have written my own willful way:
Dear Lord, forgive!

If I have written idle words or vain,
If I have worked for earthly gain,
If my words should bring one soul pain,
Dear Lord, forgive!

If I appropriated words not mine,
If I failed to give a credit line,
If I've cast my pearls before swine,
Dear Lord, forgive!

If I've failed in substance or in style,
If in anything I've stooped to guile,
If I've failed at all to win your smile,
Dear Lord, forgive!

Forgive the sins I have confessed to you,
Forgive the sins I don't know I do,
And make my writing both good and true,
And all else forgive.

Amen.

To Proceed in This Labor

(written by Samuel Johnson on the day he signed a contract to write the first complete dictionary of the English language)

O God, who hast hitherto supported me,
enable me to proceed in this labor,
and in the whole task of my present state;
that when I shall render up, at the last day,
an account of the talent committed to me,
I may receive pardon,
for the sake of Jesus Christ. Amen.

Of Making Many Books

Lord God, I have no desire to add to the endless supply of books (Ecclesiastes 12:12). There are so many great books that I–and others–have yet to read. I don't want to write anything that would be a mere distraction from such gems.

But if there is something you want to say, in a new way, maybe, I would love to be a part of that. If you would reveal to me what (if anything) YOU want me to contribute by way of the written word, then I am listening, Lord. I am all ears. I am alert and, by your grace, I am ready.

Acceptable in Your Sight

(based on Psalm 19:14)

Let the meditation of my heart,
Every thought of my mind,
Each word my fingers write,
Be acceptable in your sight,
O Lord, my strength and my redeemer.

Schedule

Lord, help me to schedule my writing well
and so defend against chaos and whim.[2]

Help me to plan my writing well
that I might have ample time for reflection,
research, and
revision.

Help me to keep to a healthy writing routine
so that my senses and skills
will be sharpened and honed.

Make my writing calendar
"a net for catching days,"[3]
and inspiration
and revelation,
in Jesus' name, amen.

[2]Phrase borrowed from Annie Dillard, *The Writing Life* (San Francisco: Harper & Row, 32).
[3]Ibid.

Spark

Lord, today and every day,
spark my writing;
Make it electric.
Inject it with life,
and infuse it with flavor.
Make my thoughts clear,
my ideas sharp,
my words strong,
and their impact life-changing,
in Jesus' name, amen.

A Capable Writer

Lord, make me a capable writer,
an inspiring communicator,
a wordsmith,
a story-crafter,
a truth-teller,
hope-instiller,
life-changer,
question-asker,
need-filler,
thrill-giver,
chill-giver,
funnybone-tickler,
tear-jerker,
page-turner,
strength-supplier,
spirit-lifter,
love-spreader,
friend-of-God-maker
kind of writer,
in Jesus' name, amen.

Keyboard Prayer

Lord God, my Father, my King,
my Sovereign, my All,
I RETURN to you with all my heart,
I ENTER your presence with gratitude and joy,
I ESCAPE into your arms and nestle in the shadow of your wing.

DELETE the stain of worldly strife and wicked desires.
SHIFT my attention and priorities to reflect your wishes.
COMMAND me and bend me to your will.
CONTROL my impulse, intellect, and intentions
until I see no OPTION
and pursue no FUNCTION
but that which is utterly and constantly
pleasing to you,
in Jesus' name, amen.

Lay Down

Lord, I lay myself down,
on this page,
in these words,
lines,
thoughts,
ideas,
hopes,
and dreams.

As you laid down your life
and raised it up again,
make something living
of my simple,
poor,
tiny
offering.

Amen.

A Writer's Senses

Gracious God,
thank you for the smell of pencil shavings,
the elegance of a good fountain pen,
and the click-clack of ancient typewriter keys...
for the intoxication of creative juices,
the sweetness of a well-turned phrase...
for the creak of the office chair,
and the surprise of a catch in the throat
and the salty track of a tear on the cheek...
for the hum of a computer,
for the thrum of a printer,
for the agony of the blank page,
the ecstasy of the last line,
the terror of hitting "send"
and the fragrance of fresh ink on crisp new pages.
Thank you, Lord, for these gifts and graces,
and for the many others I am too dull to sense,
in Jesus' name, amen.

Remind Me

Lord, remind me
when inspiration fails me and writing is a slog,
that even at such times
the writing life is a life of privilege and blessing.

Remind me
when I feel overwhelmed with work
of the "dry spells" I've endured
when paying jobs were few.

Remind me
when I am tempted to do less than my best
to make every word, sentence, paragraph, and page
a holy offering to you.

Remind me
when I feel like goofing off online
that I used to hope for the joy and honor
of being a writer.

Remind me
when the bank account dwindles and the budget tightens,
that you are my provider,
not publishers, contracts, and royalties,
in Jesus' name, amen.

Two Quatrains

Let my writing be a blessing.
Let my words all ring true,
and both victory and failure
bring glory, Lord, to you;

Let what I write and how I write it
reflect all you mean to me
while also giving pleasure
and changing those who read.

A Weak Writer's Prayer

Abba,
I am a weak writer:
insecure,
inadequate,
in over my head.
But you chose Ehud because of his weakness.
You used him,
not to mention Moses, David, Jeremiah, Paul, and others
(though I did just mention them; see what I mean?).
So grant me the faith
to believe that you can choose me and use me too.
Give me the perseverance to labor in obscurity
and keep on working and growing and developing,
even in the dark.
Help me to write in all my weakness,
in vulnerability,
bruised and broken,
in tears,
crippled,
in poverty and pain,
waiting for your strength and your timing,
in Jesus' name, amen.

Why I Write

To know what otherwise I would not know,[4]
To go where otherwise I may not go;
To feel, to learn, to grow, to see,
Become what otherwise I could not be;
Remember, reminisce, repent,
Restore a bit of what I've spent,
Recapture what I miss and, too,
Envision what I'd like to do;
Escape, sometimes, and heal my mind,
Revive my heart, explore, refine,
Obey your call, fulfill your will,
And sense your smile, and let you fill
And flood my soul with truth and light–
That and more is why I write.

[4]Adapted from William Shakespeare's *Love's Labour's Lost*, I.1.5.

A Writer's Breastplate

(based on the Breastplate of St. Patrick)

I bind to myself today
The strong Name of the Trinity,
Invoking the same,
The Three in One
and One in Three.

I plead for my thinking and writing today
The power of love, the power of faith,
Christ's incarnate immanence,
The passion of his holy death,
Awareness of His imminence,
His power bursting from the spiced tomb,
His exaltation up the heavenly way,
His princely coming at the day of doom
I plead for them all today.

I invoke for my words the power
Of angels' shout,
The sweet 'Well done' in judgment hour,
The voice of the seraphim,
The certainty of the Apostles,
The backbone of patriarchs,
The certainty of prophets,
And all good work done
as to the Lord and not for men.

I ask for my work today
The virtues of the starlit heaven,
The glorious sun's lifegiving ray,
The whiteness of the moon at even,
The flashing of the lightning free,
The whirling wind's tempestuous shocks,
The stable earth, the deep salt sea
Around the old eternal rocks.

I beseech for my sentences, paragraphs, and pages,
My grammar, style, usage, and punctuation,
My concepts and conceits, advances and retreats,
The power of God to inspire and lead,
His eye to watch, His might to stay,
His ear to hearken to my need.
The wisdom of my God to teach,
His hand to guide, His shield to ward;
The word of God to give them speech,
His heavenly host to be their guard.

Against the demon snares of sin,
The lie of judgment, lack of grace,
The haunting doubts that war within,
The lazy word, the easy phrase,
Such fatal flaws as these in me,
In every place and in all hours,
Against all unChristlike tendencies
I ask, in Jesus' name, these powers.

Against all Satan's spells and wiles,
Against false words of heresy,
Against the knowledge that defiles,
Against the heart's idolatry,

Against the world's deceitful thrills,
Against the lure of pleasing men,
Against dependence on my own skills,
Protect me, Christ, as you alone can.

Christ be with me, be all to me,
Christ behind me, Christ before me,
Christ beside me, Christ flow through me,
Christ to empty and restore me.
Christ my waking, Christ my sleeping,
Christ my thinking, Christ my feeling,
Christ my laughing, Christ my weeping,
Christ concealing and revealing.

I ask all this in the Name,
The strong Name of the Trinity,
By invocation of the same,
The Three in One and One in Three.
By Whom all nature has creation,
Eternal Father, Spirit, Word:
Praise to the Lord of my salvation,
Salvation is of Christ the Lord.
Amen.

Write Your Own Prayer

About the Author

Bob Hostetler (*www.bobhostetler.com*) is an award-winning author, literary agent, and international speaker from Ohio, who these days lives in southern Nevada.

His more than fifty books, which include the award-winning *Don't Check Your Brains at the Door* (co-authored with Josh McDowell) and the dual-timeline novel, *The Bone Box*, have sold millions of copies.

As a literary agent with the Steve Laube Agency, Bob represents the work of fiction and nonfiction writers to Christian publishers. He has been a radio disc jockey, radio commentator, game writer, pastor and preacher, and (with his wife, the lovely Robin) a foster parent to eleven teenage boys (though not all at once). He and his wife love spending time with their daughter, son, son-in-law, daughter-in-law, and their five perfect grandchildren.